KODANSHA LIBRARY OF JAPANESE ART

No. 13

Plate 1 (front cover)
COURTESAN
Detail of Plate 8.

Plate 2. KAIGETSUDO ANCHI: COURTESAN
Print, large. Former Ledoux Collection.

日
本
戯
画
懐
月
堂
安
知
図

懐 月 堂

KAIGETSUDO

(circa 1700–1750)

Edited by
TAKAHASHI SEIICHIRO

English text by
RICHARD LANE

CHARLES E. TUTTLE COMPANY
Rutland, Vermont—Tokyo, Japan

NOTE ON THE ENGLISH TEXT

*The original Japanese text to this volume, by the noted econo-
mist and ukiyo-e connoisseur Dr. Takahashi Seiichiro, deals in
some detail with the social and economic background of the
eighteenth century, together with early Japanese misconceptions
regarding the Kaigetsudo painters. In this the first monograph
on the school in a Western language, I have thought it advis-
able, both in the text and in the plates, to approach the subject
entirely anew—consolidating our present knowledge of the group,
indicating what problems remain unsolved, and attempting for
the first time to characterize the individual artists of a school
which has come to symbolize the spirit of ukiyo-e and of Toku-
gawa Japan.*

*Japanese names are given surname first in the Japanese style
throughout. Since it is difficult to keep track of the wanderings
of paintings and prints from one private collection to another,
I have most often retained here the ownership notices of the
original Japanese edition. The prints marked "Former Ledoux
Collection" are now in the Metropolitan Museum of Art, New
York; I retain the old annotation in the memory of a great
collector.*

Asakusa, Tokyo   *R. L.*

Published by the Charles E. Tuttle Company, of Rutland, Vermont
& Tokyo, Japan, by arrangement with Kodansha, Tokyo. All rights
reserved by Kodansha, without whose written permission no part of
the contents of this book may be reproduced.

First English edition, 1959

Library of Congress Catalog Card No. 59-6633

Printed in Japan
by Dai Nippon Printing Co., Tokyo

THE KAIGETSUDO PAINTERS

My love is gone somewhere
beyond the Komagata Shrine—
Weep, o cuckoo-bird!

—Takao, courtesan of the Yoshiwara

CLOSE BY the bank of the Sumida River, just south of the famed Komagata Shrine and equidistant between the *sumo* arena at Kuramae and the great Kannon Temple of Asakusa, lies a district of Tokyo that was known until recent times as Suwa-cho. The name derives from the Suwa Shrine that still guards the quarter. Wartime bombings have levelled the old shrine to the ground, but still the children of Asakusa play in its now-tiny precincts, oblivious to the hue and clamor of the tradesmen in the surrounding toy and ornament manufacturing district.

This is the center of Asakusa, in its turn, one of the centers of Old Edo. Daily, in former times, the rakes and dandies of fashionable Edo took this road as they wended their way to the Yoshiwara, a mile or so to the north. And here, just a stone's throw from the local shrine, the Kaigetsudo artists created, some 250 years ago, a glowing record of the fair women of Old Edo that thrills us even to this day.

THE PAINTINGS. Except for some two- or three-dozen prints, issued by three different publishers sometime during the 1710's, the entire output of the Kaigetsudo school is in the form of paintings. Though often referred to erroneously as "oil paintings, on silk," the work of the Kaigetsudo group was done entirely in "body colors," heavy, rather subdued water colors, and most commonly on strong Japanese paper. The paintings were nearly always mounted as kakemono, vertical scrolls to be hung in an alcove especially constructed for that purpose.

The earliest ukiyo-e, the great genre screens of the early seventeenth century, were of course entirely painted, for the art of the popular woodblock print had yet to develop. The work of Moronobu, the first great consolidator of the ukiyo-e style, was primarily in the field of book illustration, but included a certain number of prints and, particularly in his later years, paintings. It is not infrequent in the history of ukiyo-e to find a master in his later years thus abandoning popular prints and illustration work for the more difficult but more prestigious work of painting for wealthy patrons. The Kaigetsudo group and Eishi come to mind immediately as artists who are known today in the West for their prints but who considered themselves primarily painters. Miyagawa Choshun, who deserves a place among the greatest genre painters in Japanese history, is practically unknown in the West: he painted ukiyo-e all his life, but never designed a single print. No book on ukiyo-e fails to include a lengthy discussion of the Kaigetsudo prints—with only the footnote "they also did paintings."

The present volume, with some eight prints and twenty-six paintings (not including details), attempts to correct this erroneous impression. Yet even so the prints are out of proportion to their actual place in the Kaigetsudo canon, for they represent, after all, but a temporary experiment on the part of three of the founder's pupils. Despite the numbers in which the prints were manufactured, there are only thirty-nine of them extant today, in a total of twenty-two designs. The paintings of the Kaigetsudo group, though produced, of course, only in single copies, are today extant in well over a hundred works.

THE PRINTS. We may state without exaggeration that the only reason why the Kaigetsudo, a school of painters unsurpassed in their day, are known in the West is because one year they issued, quite as a sideline, two or three sets of woodblock prints. These prints, of which twenty-two designs of a probable several dozen are now extant, are sought by collectors the world over, and each brings prices up to three thousand dollars on the rare occasions when they appear on the market. At the time they were issued, these prints sold for less than a reproduction costs today.

The Kaigetsudo paintings, however, which probably represented several full days' work by a skilled painter, now sell for two to five hundred dollars, which probably represents only about three to four times what the painter actually got for them. The reason for this disparity in current values lies largely in the fact that Japanese prints are now in fashion, whereas paintings are not. At the same time it cannot be denied that, whatever their original cheapness, the Kaigetsudo prints are great prints, exploiting to the fullest the potentialities of the black-and-white woodblock technique. Why the Kaigetsudo prints did not appeal to the audience of their own day as much as did the paintings is not clear, but the reason possibly lies in the fact that the market for courtesan pictures was still a largely affluent one, whereas the commoners (including women) who bought the inexpensive prints were more interested in depictions of the actors, whom they could actually see "in the flesh," than in the courtesans, who were the product of a special world far beyond their reach. In this sense, Kaigetsudo's painted beauties were "pin-ups" only for the wealthy connoisseur. It was to be several decades before prints of beautiful girls came to challenge the actor prints for supremacy in the "low-cost field."

We must add that, whatever their popular reception, the artistic success of the Kaigetsudo prints was not a matter of chance; behind them lay the rich tradition which had been established by the master painter Kaigetsudo Ando—a tradition which, though based on colors and brush, was eminently suited to transference to the medium of the woodblock print. The massive contours of Ando's paintings (a style which, whatever its debt to shrine paintings and the founders of ukiyo-e, we must consider basically a creation of Ando) could be transferred directly to the block; in place of the magnificent coloring, masses of black and intricate but boldly patterned designs could be effectively substituted. Often, further, suggestive coloring could be applied by hand, and several of the extant Kaigetsudo prints are of the *tan-e* variety, black-and-white prints with simple coloring added by hand.

The present price of Kaigetsudo prints (the highest in the field) is doubtless due, in part, to their rarity; their remarkable qualities as prints, however, are another matter again. There is no need to try to rate comparatively the courtesan prints of Moronobu, Sugimura, Kiyonobu, Kiyomasu, and Kaigetsudo; each is great in its way. Yet of all these artists it is the Kaigetsudo alone that has come to stand as the ever-recurring symbol of ukiyo-e and of this Golden Age of Japanese culture. The Kaigetsudo prints stand independent because they are not illustrations of some scene or depictions of some famous actor in a given role. These solitary women exist for themselves alone, characteristic of, yet standing clearly apart from the world that bore them. And here, as we pay homage to these prints that mark one of the pinnacles of ukiyo-e, we must not forget the man who begot them. The prints are signed Anchi, Doshin, Dohan, but before each name we find the inscription "Follower of Kaigetsu." It is, indeed, the genius of Kaigetsudo Ando that stands behind each of these prints. It was he who set the style and taught the principles: without him these prints could not have been.

(For the prints, see Plates 2, 3, 6, 7, 9, 10, 11, and 12; the other illustrations to this volume are of paintings.)

THE ARTISTS. Although it is now generally recognized that each of the names employed by the Kaigetsudo group repre-

sents a different, individual artist, no attempt has been made, even in Japan, to characterize these individuals. Even aside from the obvious similarities between the pupils of Ando, the simple physical problem of studying all of the paintings and prints in the widely scattered collections of the world remains an almost insurmountable one.

Some such attempt must be made, however, both to justify the assertion of individual authorship, and to clarify the unified yet nevertheless individual style of the members of the school. It may also be of interest to record the number of extant paintings and prints that I have been able to trace to date. These numbers include all of the prints known (though even here we may hope a new one will turn up any day), and all of the paintings which I have been able to see or obtain photographs of—perhaps ninety percent of the Kaigetsudo work extant. I will include also similar information on the later painters in the Kaigetsudo style, and try— for the first time—to group these according to the relative degrees of influence that may be discerned.

Fakes (which are numerous) have of course been eschewed, though from photographs it is sometimes difficult to spot a forged signature or seal—occasionally added by dealers to genuine, but unsigned paintings. The discussion has been related, so far as possible, to works illustrated in this volume, though another hundred plates would have been necessary for a really comprehensive showing of the Kaigetsudo group. The serious student of the Kaigetsudo painters must also learn to differentiate the styles of calligraphy involved in the signatures, but I have had to omit a consideration of this problem, as it would necessarily involve extensive extra illustration.

I. KAIGETSUDO ANDO (traditional dates, 1671–1743). The founder of the Kaigetsudo school, Ando, was active from sometime shortly after 1700 to the year 1714 when, for reasons we'll discuss later, he was forced to abandon his work and leave Edo. Ando's family name is recorded variously as Okazaki and Okazawa, and his given name as Genshichi. From his earliest period as a painter, however, he employed the given name Ando (also pronounced Yasunori or Yasunobu and sometimes misread "Ankei"), and the studio name Kaigetsudo (pronounced "ki-gets-doh"). The latter name means "embrace-the-moon studio," referring, doubtless, to the Zen monk who is so often depicted in paintings, pointing his finger at the moon—thus indicating his essential identity with that celestial body.

Ando was an artist of Edo (the present Tokyo), living in the Suwa-cho district of Asakusa. Site of the great Kannon Temple since very early times, Asakusa was (as it is today) in a sense the epitome of Edo, the center of the new, plebeian renaissance. It had been the home of such popular heroes as Banzuiin Chobei and Sukeroku—both, the "Robin Hoods" of their day, and still immortalized in the Kabuki theatre. Asakusa had a history and a tradition; it was to be the birthplace of much of the culture of Edo.

Asakusa had also, at its northern extremity, the Yoshiwara, the district of the famed demimonde of Edo and the haunt of the literati as well as of rakes and vagabonds. The Yoshiwara had also some two thousand women, including, we need not doubt, some of the fairest in all Japan. Our painter Ando lived a little more than a mile south of this famed quarter, directly on the main road to and from the Yoshiwara.

From a consideration of Ando's broad, majestic manner of painting, each work standing as though it were framed and set up in a shrine, it has been suggested that his early training may have been in painting *ema,* votary tablets with large pictures of horses, warriors, and such, which were contributed to temples and shrines as offerings. Ando's residence, practically next door to the famed Suwa and Komagata shrines, and only a half-mile south of the great Asakusa Kannon Temple, certainly fits well with this surmise. Clearly his manner of painting with thick outlines and majestic poses owes much to *ema*, though this powerful style is combined with a grace and artistic sense that was partly his own contribution and partly derived, doubtless, from the works of such predecessors as Moronobu and Sugimura.

At any rate it is clear that daily in front of Ando's shop passed the tourists, rakes, and literati on their way to and from the Kannon Temple and the Yoshiwara. Whether he was a painter of temple *ema* or simply an aspiring painter of the genre scene, from some impulse Ando began taking as his special subject the beauties of the Yoshiwara, and soon, his fame spreading, he came almost to monopolize the field of courtesan painting.

Although the early eighteenth century was the period of the first widespread manufacture of Japanese ukiyo-e prints, it must be remembered that the prints were cheap in price, and hardly considered more than souvenirs, not works of art. Each Japanese house had, however, a tokonoma alcove for the express purpose of hanging a kakemono painting. To the frequenter (or would-be frequenter) of the Yoshiwara, nothing would be more natural than to substitute for the traditional landscape or calligraphic scroll the painting of his favorite girl. The Kaigetsudo paintings were indeed glorified "pin-ups."

One does not have to read the language to find out that the courtesan was a pretty important person in the social life of old Japan: that fact will be obvious even from a casual glance at the art of the period. The Japanese male, his marriage prearranged for him by his parents while he was still in puberty, needed some outlet for the urges of romance and adventure that fill any normal male. High adventure was well-nigh impossible, for the land was ruled by a strict military dictatorship, travel outside Japan was punishable by death, and for a townsman, whatever his wealth, to raise himself into the more glamorous samurai society was a feat but rarely accomplished. The townsman's only area for ad-

Plate 6. KAIGETSUDO DOSHIN: COURTESAN
Print, large. Former Ledoux Collection.

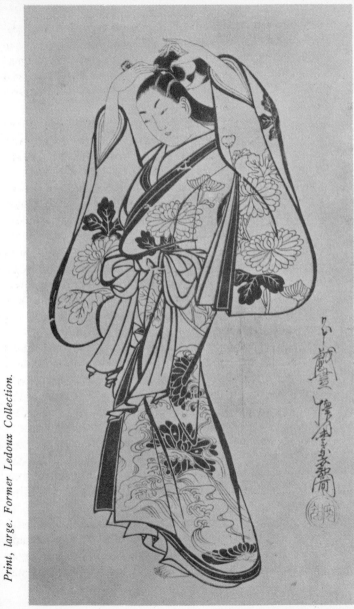

Plate 7. KAIGETSUDO ANCHI: COURTESAN
Print, large. *Former Ledoux Collection.*

venturous self-expression lay in the making of money and the spending of it—the latter principally in the courtesan district where, though love was largely an item of commerce, a man was at least free to choose his own sweetheart and even, if he could afford it, reserve her for his own exclusive pleasure.

So it was that following the establishment in each of the major Japanese cities of licensed quarters, these districts, with their highly trained and educated courtesans, soon became the acknowledged centers of male social life, the haunt of connoisseurs and literati, as well as of rakes and lovers. During the first half of the seventeenth century, the higher levels of this pleasure-bent society were apparently dominated by the more wealthy samurai. But from the mid seventeenth century it was the townsman who came gradually to reign supreme. And, with the continued rise of a mercantile economy, the average samurai became more and more improverished, and unable to afford such costly pleasures. Thus from the 1660's onwards, the demimonde became almost a monopoly of the middle- and upper-class townsman.

With, then, these new centers of pleasure and refined entertainment set up in the cities of Japan, there arose a large body of literature and art, produced almost exclusively for the purpose of amusing or celebrating this world. The literature was a type of gay novel that came to be called *ukiyo-zoshi*, or "fleeting-world booklets"; Saikaku is the best-known of the authors, but he had many contemporaries and followers. On the artistic side, the result of this "renaissance of gaiety" was the ukiyo-e, or "fleeting-world pictures"; the master of the artists who specialized exclusively in the courtesan was Kaigetsudo Ando.

In a world where money reigned supreme, it was only natural that the more strong-willed of the courtesans should develop certain standards of their own in judging a lover, or would-be lover. This quality of will-power and integrity was to play an important part in forming the average townsman's attitude toward the courtesan. She could be had, theoretically, for money; at the same time, a guest who tried to force himself upon a courtesan would be considered a *yabo*, or "crude boor," and become the laughing stock of the gay quarter. The Japanese courtesan was thus at once a prostitute and not a prostitute. She was, indeed, bought for money; but at the same time she enjoyed a considerable degree of freedom and influence in her own limited world. It .was this unique quality that was to make the Japanese courtesan (at once resembling and differing from the ancient Greek hetaera) the subject and the impulse for a vast body of surprisingly high-quality literature and art, that was to sustain itself for nearly three hundred years.

If anything, the art which celebrated the courtesan tended to be more subtle, more universal, than the literature; and this is surely the reason why the masterpieces of the Kaigetsu-do artists are revered by connoisseurs the world over, whereas the literature, even when translated. appeals only to a small audience of lovers of the exotic. Much of the literature identified its courtesan heroines by name and house; on not one of the Kaigetsudo pictures do we find any patent guide to identification. Nevertheless, the paintings and prints most probably do depict the reigning beauties of the day, but in an idealized, timeless form, with only an occasional characteristic trait of kimono pattern or stance to indicate what girl was actually portrayed.

We have, of course, in Western art a school of portraiture specializing in full-length portraits of fair ladies, these paintings most often of specific, eminent personages. For the equivalent of the Japanese *bijin-ga*—paintings and prints of beautiful girls as the focal point for a vast, semi-popular, semi-erotic art form—we must perhaps turn to the nude in Western painting.

The nude, it happens, never developed as a separate form

in Japanese art; the emphasis of female beauty lay always on the facial features, the long raven hair, and the kimono. Certainly it cannot be denied that the elaborate Japanese kimono was a work of art in itself, well worthy of preservation by the more graphic arts. Perhaps more than in any other country, however, the dress came to form a most vital factor in the appreciation of feminine beauty. The matter was stated very plainly by the courtesan Naoe of the Shimmachi pleasure quarter in Osaka. At the time of the Kansei Reforms of 1789 and following—a time when the government was attempting to restrict all luxuries—this redoubtable courtesan sent in a strong protest to the authorities against the ban on rich kimonos. Her words were, in part, "Our world is different from the ordinary world. ... If we were to dress ourselves just like ordinary girls, how on earth could we manage to attract lovers!"

Thus it is that in order really to enjoy the Kaigetsudo paintings to the fullest degree, one must develop something of the Japanese love and appreciation for the kimono as a work of art. And works of art these are indeed: one has only to glance at such paintings as those reproduced in Plates 5 and 17, for example, to see that there is something more here than a simple girl; there is—can we say—a whole culture involved in the appreciation of even one such painting. In the hands of a master such as Ando, the individual courtesan can somehow rise above the overpowering grandeur of the kimono and impress the viewer with her human, erotic charm. With several of Ando's pupils and followers, however, the painting often stands or falls upon the beauty and originality of the robes alone.

The Genroku period of the late seventeenth and early eighteenth centuries (to the latter part of which the Kaigetsu-do paintings belong) marks, it should be noted, a definite pinnacle in the development of the woman's kimono as a work of art. It was, indeed, during this very period that the

This view, indeed, was that held by several of the early students of ukiyo-e in the West. They had not seen more than a few of the paintings, and had no chance to discern the slight, but nevertheless distinct, differences that mark both the painting style and the calligraphy of each member of the Kaigetsudo school. In the present volume I have tried to suggest some of the distinguishing characteristics visible after a careful study of the different members of the school. As, however, in the case of distinguishing, say, the style of Botticelli from that of his contemporary imitators, it is sometimes only an impression of quality and greatness, rather than a particular twist of lip or eyebrow, that makes all the difference in an attribution.

If a single criterion were to be given for distinguishing the work of the master Ando from the Kaigetsudo pupils, it would inevitably involve the observation of a certain lessening of strength in the latter, a tendency toward "prettiness." The calligraphy expert will note similar tendencies in the handwriting of the signatures. The format of these pupils' signatures most often includes the phrase *Kaigetsu matsuyo*, followed by the personal name (Anchi, Doshin, Doshu, Doshiu, or Dohan) in handwriting, and usually in the seal. Sometimes, however, the seal of the master Ando appears after the signature of a pupil. The artists probably worked in the actual atelier of the master, and the presence of his seal on their paintings doubtless indicates, in the Japanese tradition, that Ando thought them worthy of representing his school. Although there exists no data to assist in definitely dating the paintings and prints, it is quite possible that the Kaigetsudo pupils continued, occasionally, to use the master's seal in memoriam even after his exile; possibly he bequeathed it to them when he departed from Edo.

The principal problem in the signatures of the pupils is the phrase *Kaigetsu matsuyo*, just noted. Literally, the phrase means "descendant of Kaigetsudo." *Matsuyo* (also

Plate 11. KAIGETSUDŌ DOHAN: COURTESAN
Print, large. *Former Ledoux Collection.*

Plate 12. KAIGETSUDO DOHAN: COURTESAN
Print, large. Former Ledoux Collection.

pronounced *batsuyo*) has the secondary meanings of "the future life, posterity, all ages to come, eternity." This fact has misled some Western students to the supposition that it might mean "Kaigetsudo's last years." The word refers, however, to humanity in general, not to the individual existence.

The term, in either connotation, does not seem to appear in the signature of any other painter of this or any other period, though it is obviously related to the expression *Hishikawa yo* (follower of Hishikawa) used by Moronobu's pupil Moroshige but a decade or two earlier. It is clearly a special usage, impossible to define literally, outside of its context; nevertheless, it definitely implies "descendant," or "in the lineage of." It does not itself mean "pupil," but under the Japanese system of adoption of pupils by a master, such might well be implied. So far as the terminology goes, at any rate, the later paintings are simply "in the lineage of the Kaigetsu Studio," most probably by pupils related, by blood or by adoption, to the master. Ando's surname does not appear on any of his works, only the name of his studio, Kaigetsudo. Thus both he and his school became known by the name of his studio.

The only real context for the language is, of course, the paintings and prints themselves. A careful study reveals distinct differences in style between each of the painters of the Kaigetsudo school, as will be made clear in the discussion that follows.

As might only be expected in the work of the founding genius of a school, the paintings of Kaigetsudo Ando display an originality, a strength and freshness, which is seldom mirrored with perfection even in the work of his finest pupils. At the same time, Ando's courtesans often display a certain austere yet thoughtful mien which tends to remove them from the realm of simple "pin-up girls"—the objects of plainly erotic attention.

The genuine paintings of Ando that I have before me as

I write—a few originals, but mainly photographs—number twenty-eight or nearly twice the number extant for any of his pupils. In addition we must include at least a dozen unsigned works (see Plate 32, for example), that seem clearly to bear the distinguishing marks of the master. One fact that will be apparent to anyone examining these paintings after coming from the works of his pupils, is the great variety of Ando's poses. Some of these poses are, indeed, to recur often in the imitations of his pupils (compare Plates 17 and 34, for example). Many of them, however, appear in no artist but Ando.

With one exception to be noted subsequently in the case of Anchi, the extant works of Ando's pupils show little variation from the theme of the single standing courtesan. Such is far from being the case with Ando. Fully half a dozen of the paintings of his that have survived the earthquakes, fires, and bombings of Japan display a mastery of group genre-painting technique that goes well beyond the narrow confines for which he is most famous. The painting we reproduce in Plates 14 and 15 is worthy of a Moronobu or a Hokusai: it displays a skill in group composition and a wit and movement that are only hinted at in the customary courtesan paintings. Yet even if such unusual paintings as this were no longer exant, we could discern from Ando's paintings of smaller, more traditional groups of twos and threes (Plates 13 and 33, for example), that his genius extended far beyond the single standing figure. Among other examples of Ando's versatility we might mention his extensive picture-scroll illustrating the Oeyama-Shutendoji legend, and his several boudoir scenes wherein we find a skilled placement of the courtesan amidst the bedding and the mosquito net—accoutrements later to be widely employed by Utamaro, who, indeed, we might well call the Kaigetsudo of his generation.

Ando's women are not of one type alone. We have mentioned already the austere, stately figures, more goddesses than objects of sexual attention. Plates 4, 13, and 16 are typical of these women. But there is yet another girl in Ando's work, a girl much more of our own world, who may be appreciated without such great submersion in Japanese taste. We find this girl most strikingly in Plate 17, again in Plate 32. Hers is a willowy, sinuous figure which belies the weight of the fine robes wrapped about her; she stands detached, yet somehow intimate and approachable, a girl one would go a long way to meet. Others of Ando's women (and those of most of his pupils) stand somewhere between these two extremes: they are more feminine than the first, less lovable than the last. Judging from numbers, however, it was the aloof, goddess-like beauty that struck the taste of the Edo connoisseurs of Ando's time, and it remained for Suke-nobu, Ando's great contemporary in Kyoto, fully to exploit the theme of this lovable "girl next door."

We have characterized the general style (or styles) of Ando; further comments will be found appended to each of the plates reproducing Ando's work: 4, 8, 13, 14 and 15, 16, 17, 18, 32, and 33. To go any further, we must first examine the work and style of each of his pupils, seeing what each brought to, or lost from, the style created by the founder.

II. CHOYODO ANCHI. Anchi (also pronounced Yasutomo), like the other four immediate pupils of Ando, often employed the studio name Kaigetsudo. On other occasions, however, he used the name Choyodo, meaning "long-the-sun studio," and doubtless having special connotations derived from Kaigetsudo, "embrace-the-moon studio." Anchi is the only immediate Kaigetsudo pupil to have a studio name of his own; he is also the only pupil to derive his given name from the first syllable of Ando's name: all of the other four pupils begin their names with the "do" element. Whatever their exact significance, these facts do indicate that Anchi
(continued on page 72)

Plate 13 (see following page for caption)

Plate 13 (preceding page)
KAIGETSUDO ANDO: COURTESAN WITH SERVANT GIRL
Painting in colors on paper, large. Tokyo National Museum.

In rhythmical unity the courtesan leans over, her arm about the
little girl's shoulder, doubtless whispering some advice about men;
for the little apprentice will herself become a courtesan before
too many years have passed. The straight figure of the little girl
supports a sharply delineated pattern of ivy leaves; the courtesan's
pliant figure displays a more subdued design of bamboo-grass laden
with snow.

Plates 14 & 15 (detail)
KAIGETSUDO ANDO: SHOKI KIDNAPPING A COURTESAN
Painting in colors on paper, large. Kaburagi Kiyokata Collection.

Opinions vary as to the meaning of this painting, but all critics
agree to its unusuality in a school dominated by the standing figure
of the lone courtesan. The mythological figure Shoki is known as
the "demon-queller," and traditional Chinese and Japanese paintings depict him in that function. By the eighteenth century, however, he (a traditional woman-hater) came sometimes to be
depicted by artists in rather compromising situations.

Here too, though the painting is traditionally entitled "Shoki
Saving a Courtesan from a Devil," it is obvious that something
is wrong. Shoki is saving her, all right, but for himself! While his
traditional enemy helps him pack off his prize, Shoki beats off the
townsmen who come after with stick and rope to retrieve the
complaisant local beauty whom the "demon-queller" has snatched.

Note the skillful composition, drawn together, as it were, by
the powerful, outstretched hand of the bearded hero.

KAIGETSUDO ANDO: COURTESAN
Painting in colors on paper, large. Nakamura Gakuryo Collection.

The same artist, but back again to his true metier! A cool, graceful beauty, standing (in the mind's eye, at least) amidst the windblown grasses of autumn. For, it will be noted, the Kaigetsudo paintings have no background, and hardly any props. The girl and the kimono are all. Yet, even to the sophisticated urbanite of Old Edo, the seasons still retained their importance; and the artist never forgot that fact as he went about the intricate task of designing a new kimono for each painting.

It not infrequently happens that some of us, oversaturated with art, may come to prefer the painted flower, the painted woman, to the real thing. The Kaigetsudo paintings carry this idea one step further, and we are asked to visualize Nature's beauty as reproduced by the artist from the robe of a courtesan. This is indeed stylized Nature, rarified sex; but highly satisfying in the hands of a master!

The Kaigetsudo prints are customarily in the *kakemono-e* size, about twelve by twenty-three inches. The paintings are even larger, averaging about eighteen inches in width and three and a half feet in length. Whereas the prints—being originally in black and white with emphasis on line—come out well in facsimile, no ordinary reproduction can do the Kaigetsudo paintings justice, either in coloring or in size. The average head alone measures about three by four inches; in Plates 18 and 19 we have tried to show two of the Kaigetsudo heads in approximately the original size, but their majestic figures can only be suggested at one-fifth scale (Plates 16 and 20)—and even here the top and bottom of the paintings (blank paper, but still a part of the composition) have had to be cropped. (Plate 8 will give some idea of the total length, and of the kakemono mounting. The original is four feet high and, as is characteristic of the Kaigetsudo paintings, appears almost life-size when viewed from a few feet away.)

Plate 17
KAIGETSUDO ANDO: COURTESAN
Painting in colors on paper, large. Tokyo National Museum.

We've seen this particular kimono pattern, the "steel-wire lotus" (clematis), already in Plates 4 and 5. Here, despite the beauty of the girl's face, hair, and figure, it is even more the design of the outer robe, half slipping from her shoulders, that dominates the painting. The Kaigetsudo girls are often termed "stout," or "robust"; in this painting, however, we are allowed to glimpse that the girl beneath the layers of kimono is a frail thing after all, slim and pliant, more shy and pensive than actually aloof.

Enveloped in the atmosphere of that almost oppressively beautiful robe, we are drawn as males to a feminine loveliness that neither positively beckons nor absolutely rejects. We wish to possess her simply "because she is there." This painting surely represents one of the peaks of *bijin-ga* art in any country.

Practically the only documentary evidence we possess regarding the names of the Kaigetsudo artists is the signatures and seals on the paintings and prints themselves. The paintings of the master Ando (he designed no prints) are sometimes signed simply "Kaigetsudo," with the vermillion seal "Ando." In most cases, however, the signature is "Nippon giga Kaigetsudo," with the name Ando either signed or in the seal—often both. The words *Nippon giga* (also pronounceable *Yamato giga*) prefixed to the artist's name mean "pleasure-pictures in the Japanese style"; the word is, in fact, nothing more than the equivalent of the term "ukiyo-e" itself. The new phrase, though itself doubtless coined by Ando, is also in the tradition of Moronobu's prefix *Yamato-eshi*, "painter in the Japanese style." With Ando, however, the word *gi* (pleasure) is prefixed, indicating that the purpose of the paintings was expressly to amuse, to be loved—much as were the very courtesans who comprised his subjects. The word *giga* (pleasure-picture) thus parallels *yujo* (pleasure-woman), the Japanese term for courtesan.

KAIGETSUDO ANCHI: COURTESAN
Painting in colors on paper, large. Takeuchi Kimpei Collection.

Where the Ando of Plate 17 was intimate, the Anchi of this painting is definitely aloof. The figure is static and unpliant, as is even the kimono pattern—cherry blossoms at shoulder and skirt, and *tachibana* (orange blossoms) at the bottom of the flowing sleeves, reminiscent, doubtless, of the twin trees that bloomed before the Imperial Palace in Kyoto. Although her name is lost, we may be justified in imagining this courtesan the "aristocrat" of the gay quarter of her day.

For facial details see Plate 19; here we clearly discern the truth of the novelist Saikaku's comments of but a generation earlier: "The popular face these days is round, the color of cherry blossoms." And again, "This indeed is the hue of cherry blossoms—this round face in the current style."

Western writers have sometimes created an aura of mystery around the fact that no one is quite sure even how the Kaigetsudo artists pronounced their names. This "mystery," however, is one common to a majority of Japanese given names, which are susceptible to two or more pronunciations. It may be said in general of this type of name that the people themselves most often pronounced their names in the softer (and longer) Japanese-style pronunciation, whereas nearly everyone else except their relatives employed the shorter, more staccato Chinese-style pronunciation. Thus to a Japanese it does not matter very much whether the founder of the Kaigetsudo school is called Ando, Yasunori, or Yasunobu: they are all the same word. The shorter pronunciation is the more common among connoisseurs in Japan today, as it probably was in Ando's time; it has natural advantages to the Western student, who will have trouble enough remembering even the short forms.

Plate 21
CHOYODO ANCHI: COURTESAN (*detail*)
Painting in colors on paper, large. Tokyo National Museum.

Her hair set in the sweeping Katsuyama style, this courtesan stands, like most of Anchi's, aloof from the world. In skill of execution and unity of mood, this painting surely ranks among this artist's masterpieces.

Unlike the work of their great contemporary Miyagawa Choshun (whose clearly delineated kimonos, painted carefully on silk, contrast sharply with the softness of his women's faces), the Kaigetsudo painters most often combine a dominant face with robes that impress through their pattern, rather than through the brilliance of their coloring. In this painting the pattern is further subdued by its poignant literary subject, symbolized by groups of evening-glory leaves and blossoms, mingled with "Genji cartwheels." This represents, indeed, the famous fourth chapter of *The Tale of Genji,* perhaps the most memorable in the whole book, wherein Prince Genji loves and loses the tragic maiden Yugao (evening-glory).

Although we are grateful for the greater detail visible, it will be obvious that—as with the cover plate to this volume—the Kaigetsudo figures must be seen in their entirety to stand as works of art. To that degree is a Kaigetsudo painting an overall symbol, rather than an individual portrait.

Though it is a fact little realized in the West, there are today many more collectors of the actual kimonos of Kaigetsudo's day than there are of the paintings themselves. And the prices are correspondingly higher for the dresses than for the pictures of them.

Plate 22

CHOYODO ANCHI: COURTESAN
Painting in colors on paper, large. Tokyo National Museum.

Here is Anchi again, in an even more brilliant display of beauty in kimono design. Whether the Kaigetsudo painters copied extant kimono designs or invented their own is not clear, though we do know that they tended to employ larger and bolder designs than are to be found in any of the pattern-books—and other painters— of the period.

Clearly, at any rate, it would have taken a wealthy courtesan to be able to afford to recreate in cloth a design such as this one. Not, of course, that even a skilled painter could have dashed it off in an afternoon either!

Plates 23 & 24 (detail)

KAIGETSUDO DOSHIN: COURTESAN
Painting in colors on paper, large. Takeuchi Kimpei Collection.

Although some authors take the precaution of labeling the basic Kaigetsudo subject simply as "standing woman," it seems clear that these were almost entirely courtesans, "kept" women of the Yoshiwara. The present painting probably depicts a courtesan also.

It happens, however, that the female impersonators of the Kabuki theatre employed a purple cap similar to the one depicted here— this for the purpose of hiding the fact that their forelocks had, according to law, been shaved to distinguish them more clearly from real women. Since a similar cap was used occasionally by women (from whom, indeed, the actors had borrowed it), there would seem no very good reason for arbitrarily supposing this a temporary dereliction on the part of Doshin into the theatrical world.

For details of the kimono design see Plate 24. The outer garment, half dropped from the shoulders, bears a Japanese-ivy design, while that of the under garment is of bamboo-grass and gentian.

Plate 26
KAIGETSUDO DOSHIU: COURTESAN
Painting in colors on paper, large. Tokyo National Museum.

Here again we find the favorite pattern of bamboo-grass and gentian (the crest of the famous Minamoto clan). Considerably damaged, the painting has been trimmed, rather cramping the design.

This courtesan does not simply stand, she adjusts a long hairpin in her coiffure, and the result lends a certain lightness to her heavily clad figure, directs our attention to her delicate hands and arms, even to her dainty feet. Though not too frequent among the early members of the Kaigetsudo school, this pose was to become a favorite with some of their followers, such as Takizawa Shigenobu (compare Plate 35).

In the present volume it has proved unfeasible to print macrons over the long vowels. I list below the major names where the diacritical marks have been omitted over the "*o*": Kaigetsudo, Choyodo, Tosendo, Rifudo, Hakushoken, Baioken, *matsuyo,* etc.; also the "*u*" in Rifudo, Baiyuken, Kumeido, Haryu, etc. Since the macron is vital in distinguishing the two artists "Doshu," I have employed the romanization "Doshiu" for the name bearing the long *u*. This follows, as a matter of fact, the spelling of the original in the *kana* syllabary. Note, however, that the most important "*o*'s" in the book, those of Ando, Doshin, Doshu, Doshiu, and Dohan, are all short vowels.

And while on the subject of names, it is well to note that nineteenth-century Western scholars often spelt the school name "Kwaigetsudo," retaining the archaic "kw," no longer heard in actual pronunciation. (So, too, was ukiyo-e spelled "ukiyo-ye," Eishi, "Yeishi," Edo, "Yedo," etc.) These matters may seem of but antiquarian interest, but the "kw" spelling, at least, must be remembered when one uses the index of any old book or catalogue to find references to the Kaigetsudo.

Plate 27
KAIGETSUDO DOSHU: COURTESAN
Painting in colors on paper, large. Tokyo National Museum.

In this painting, one of the finest extant works of Ando's pupils, the courtesan's outer robe is seen slipping from her shoulders as she draws it together with her right hand. The robe bears a formalized design of giant cherry blossoms in circles, and the mood is clearly that of early spring—as is the suggestive accompanying verse by Watanabe Jitokusai:

> *Her face radiant like a flower, the dew not yet dried:*
> *How many men have known the joy of passion here!*
> *A closer view—how deeply dyed this lovely blossom—*
> *We've lost our heart, and spring's come to the branch!*

Here we find the custom of the *gasan,* or verse in classical Chinese to accompany a painting, applied to a product of the "fleeting world"; the author was a stylish scholar of the time. Several Kaigetsudo paintings are extant with such *gasan* by noted scholars or calligraphers, indicating considerable intercourse between these painters and the literati of the time.

It must be emphasized that at least half of the glory of the Kaigetsudo paintings lies in their coloring—which is, however, hardly susceptible to inexpensive reproduction. For the art lover who fails to find in these paintings the qualities he admires in the prints, we can only recommend a study of the originals, examples of which are to be found in several of the major museums of the world—with an almost excessive concentration in the Tokyo National Museum, from whose collection nearly half of the reproductions in the present volume are derived.

Plate 28
BAIYUKEN KATSUNOBU: COURTESAN
(see Plate 36 for the entire painting)
Painting in colors on paper, large. Takeuchi Kimpei Collection.

Although their actual training is unknown, a dozen or more painters
of the mid eighteenth century are customarily classed among the
Kaigetsudo school. Katsunobu is one of these, though his extant
work often shows as much influence of the school of Sukenobu in
Kyoto as it does of the Kaigetsudo in Edo. (The *"yu"* of Katsunobu's studio-name is also the *"suke"* of Sukenobu; thus the entire
word "Sukenobu" is included in this painter's names—quite possibly indicating some close connection with the Kyoto master.)

Katsunobu, whose work is extant in some eight paintings, is
known to us in two rather different styles. One (represented by
paintings in the British Museum and Hyodo Tokuko collections)
is a graceful, naive, unaffected style somewhat reminiscent of
Shigenobu and eminently suited to depicting the youthful beauty
of sixteen. The other style, which we see in Plates 28 and 36,
represents a more full-blown courtesan but lacks the delicate
naivety of this painter's most charming work. With Katsunobu we
note a gradual slimming of the girl's figure, a trait which is to
characterize several of the later painters in the Kaigetsudo style,
and doubtless mirrors the changing taste of the times.

Compared with the work of the early Kaigetsudo school, the
girls of Katsunobu are unimposing, definitely just ordinary girls
of this world rather than aloof goddesses. This change itself is
significant, for it mirrors the general taste of the mid eighteenth
century, not simply the individual artist's philosophy.

Plate 29
TOSENDO RIFU: COURTESAN
(see Plate 37 for the entire painting)
Painting in colors on paper, large. Tokyo National Museum.

Another of the lesser figures of the later Kaigetsudo school is Rifu, whose figures display in general a certain somberness of costume and mien. The courtesan here covers the gaudiness of her red-flowered kimono with a deep purple robe, which yet displays an intricate, though almost invisible, flower pattern. Such devices, here mirrored by the painter, were doubtless occasioned more by the austerity edicts of the Shogun Yoshimune (ruled 1716–45), than by any lessening in the desire for gaiety and color on the part of the citizens of Edo.

Plate 40 below shows a painting which, though it displays considerable differences in style from the above work of Rifu, is probably by the same painter, done at a different period of his life. The less finished style doubtless indicates earlier composition, though the painting, with the cursive Japanese syllabary written across the kimono, is in some ways more spontaneous and appealing than the later work. The painting is signed "Rifu-do Kampu," the only appearance of this name, which is probably, however, but a variation of "Rifu," for the calligraphy also greatly resembles that of Rifu.

Both of Rifu's paintings bear the inscription *Yamato-eshi* (painter in the Japanese style) before the name, which may indicate that Rifu considered himself rather in the lineage of Moronobu, who instituted the phrase. By this time, however, some thirty or forty years after Moronobu's death, his style has been so assimilated and transformed by imitators that there is very little characteristic of him left in what was then considered to be "in the manner of Moronobu."

Plate 30
MATSUNO CHIKANOBU: COURTESAN
Painting in colors on paper, large. Takeuchi Kimpei Collection.

Although his girls are more sweet and less impressive than those
of the Kaigetsudo painters per se, in originality and execution of
kimono designs Chikanobu ranks with the best of the early Kaigetsudo masters. The present design is rather more complex than
Chikanobu's finest work, but his original touch is abundantly
evident in the striking pattern of cherry blossoms of several hues
floating on a swift stream.

In Plate 41 we see another—indeed, perhaps the finest—of
Chikanobu's extant works. In her right hand the courtesan holds
an iris, and on her white-and-blue kimono are written the chapter
titles of *The Tale of Genji*. A striking pattern of blue, white, and
red maple leaves adorns the sash, and above the figure a samurai
of the Kumamoto fief has inscribed a love poem.

At his finest Chikanobu ranks with the immediate pupils of
Ando. His ladies are, however, of another generation, and that
alone almost makes them of another world. His women are almost
invariably mature; there is little girlishness even in the little
servant maids he paints beside his courtesans. Yet neither are his
women matronly. They display almost invariably a slightly smiling
face, mouth curved in a U-shape. Chikanobu's women patently
carry not a thought in their heads, and doubtless reflect the
changing ideals of womanhood in the mid eighteenth century—
their light and airy faces charming, but void of any troublesome
depths. The kimonos with which Chikanobu adorns his women are,
we may repeat, among the loveliest and most elaborate in ukiyo-e,
and in this phase of his work he is fully the equal even of Ando.

Plate 31
NISHIKAWA TERUNOBU: COURTESAN
Painting in colors on paper, large. Takeuchi Kimpei Collection.

Like Katsunobu, Nishikawa Terunobu stands closer in style to the Kyoto school of Nishikawa Sukenobu than to the Kaigetsudo school, and the similarity of surname may well indicate some direct relation. Terunobu is no master of kimono design, but there is a certain naive grace to this pattern of cherry-blossom chains, upon a dark-blue ground bearing an almost invisible design of fishermen's nets.

Terunobu appears to have been well known in his time, for one of Masanobu's picture-books speaks of him as "the founder of the style of depicting a courtesan's forehead with the brow painted high." This characteristic is not so evident in the present painting as it is in others, where the women are painted with quite high foreheads. Terunobu does not seem to me a very skilled painter, but something in the swinging outlines of this figure has made the painting a favorite among Japanese art anthologists.

There are at least a dozen other minor artists often associated with the later Kaigetsudo style—Bokuryuken, Shokando, Manrido, Horyu, among others—but their styles seem more often under Moronobu or Kiyonobu influence, and it is difficult to associate them definitely with the Kaigetsudo group. Again, there is little doubt that the early Kaigetsudo school exerted considerable influence upon the styles of such contemporary masters as Choshun, Masanobu, and others. There seems, however, no need to exaggerate the numbers of the members of the school, when it is the degree of genius or talent that the outstanding artists display that really matters in evaluating the importance of the group.

Plate 32
UNSIGNED: COURTESAN
Painting in colors on paper, large. Tokyo National Museum.

Though unsigned, and in poor condition, this painting clearly belongs to the great period of the Kaigetsudo school. It may well be the work of the master himself, Ando.

The lithely twisted figure recalls Ando's masterpiece reproduced in Plate 17. The girl's act of swinging her right sleeve over and extending it to the front, serves both to reveal the line of her back and legs, and to balance the placement of both head and feet to the far left of the composition. It is a difficult feat to achieve both balance and beauty in such a basically unnatural position; of the Kaigetsudo painters few but Ando could have succeeded.

Even in the genuine works of Ando himself a certain unevenness of inspiration will be observed. Some of his paintings are unsurpassed among Japanese *bijin-ga;* others were clearly painted simply because he had a commission to fulfill. It is quite possible, of course, that Ando sometimes had his pupils finish off the time-consuming details of his kimono designs; at the same time, he would not be the only great artist who produced just passable works together with the masterpieces. In the case of a poet such works may well be destroyed before they see the cold light of day. The painter or novelist who must work for his living is often obliged to see such works pass immediately out into the world, beyond retrieve. This is eminently true of the Kaigetsudo artists, who were, in a sense, craftsmen, artisans, rather than creators of "art for art's sake." They painted to fulfill a demand; when orders were numerous they painted day and night to fill them. In slack times they doubtless amused—or supported—themselves at things having no relation to painting. It happens, for some reason or other, that many of the world's finest paintings were produced commercially, on a commission to decorate some chapel, castle, drawing-room, or tokonoma; while some of the worst paintings we know were produced simply "for art's sake."

(continued from page 36)

was somehow treated differently from the other pupils. Possibly he may have been Ando's own son, who was allowed to set up his own studio once he had acquired sufficient skill.

Of Anchi's extant paintings I have seen about seventeen. Plates 5, 19 and 20, 21, and 22 reproduce his work in this volume. Of these, only the second is signed "Kaigetsudo matsuyo Anchi," the others being "Choyodo Anchi."

Anchi's characteristic style is rather more coyly erotic than that of his master. Plate 19, which faces a detail from an Ando painting, illustrates this clearly. As with several of Anchi's paintings, the chin is partly hidden; there is— through only minor deviations in the eyes, nose, and mouth —something almost "cunning" in the girl's expression. Whereas Ando's women can often pass as maidens or ladies of quality, Anchi's girl is definitely a courtesan, lovely, but at the same time, somehow predatory. She seems definitely to be thinking only of herself; the viewer would think twice before putting his love into her hands. To one degree or another, this is the feeling one gets from each of Anchi's paintings. Quite possibly it has little to do with his own character: some of the greatest rogues have painted the sweetest girls. It does, however, indicate his own taste in women: aristocratic, self-absorbed, disdainful. Anchi probably liked cats too.

Before turning to the somewhat different mood of Anchi's prints, we must note a definite rarity by this artist: a miniature painted screen, the only such work known by a member of this school, and the only departure from the conventional standing-courtesan pose to be found among the works of Ando's pupils. This screen (Nakagawa Collection) is extant in a pair, each composed of six small panels, in excellent condition. It is of the type called *hina-byobu*, the small screens used to form a background during the Doll Festival in the third lunar month. In view of the subject matter, it

Plate 33. KAIGETSUDO ANDO: COURTESAN DRESSING A GUEST'S HAIR
Painting in colors on silk. British Museum.

is somewhat doubtful that the screen was actually so used by any little girl: more probably it was painted for some courtesan's amusement.

One of the screens shows a scene in the streets of the Yoshiwara, courtesans with their retinues promenading while several gallants and their servants watch. The other screen shows a scene inside one of the houses of assignation: in the foreground a rake plays checkers with an actor, while serving-maidens and a courtesan watch; another guest has his shoulders massaged by a blind masseur; in the background two courtesans play the samisen while a guest sings a ballad. One of the sliding doors in the background bears the signature "Kaigetsu matsuyo Anchi." The composition of each screen is excellent; there is a wit and humor evident here that is rare in the Kaigetsudo school; we may only hope that other such works by Anchi will someday be unearthed. For, however much we may feel that Anchi's single courtesans lack the grace and refinement of Ando's, the work of Anchi in the field of more earthy, plebeian genre observation, as revealed in this pair of screens, is of the highest order, not inferior to that of his contemporaries Itcho and Masanobu.

The woodblock prints of Anchi, of which some seven are extant, constitute, at the present time, his chief claim to fame among Western connoisseurs. Coming to the prints from the paintings, one always has a feeling of a loss of intimacy. Just as the enthusiast who knows only the prints may feel the paintings to be lacking in force, so do the prints seem a little harsh and impersonal coming directly after the subtle gradations, the almost personal contact that one can achieve with the artist through his paintings. (This is a difficulty in appreciation not unknown in the West, however, and the serious student of ukiyo-e must learn to enjoy both the painted and the printed line—though he may prefer not to mix the two at one sitting.)

Anchi's prints are, it is my impression, in several ways

artistically superior to his paintings. He was not, of course, a professional print designer, his few prints being but a minor experiment, probably done on some special commission. The fact is, though, that his style, somewhat too cold and unyielding for the intimacy of painting, proved eminently suited to the woodblock technique. We accept the stiffness of these "primitive" prints as one of their charms. Under the cutter's knife, the sharply feline quality of Anchi's women is blunted to a certain vapid childishness. Somehow, his faults are lost in the technique of early printmaking. (See Plates 2 and 7.)

Anchi is not, of course the only print artist of which this is true; such ukiyo-e greats as Harunobu and Buncho, for example, were only mediocre painters. We have, unfortunately, no prints by the founder of the Kaigetsudo school, Ando. If we had, I think his prints would be the greatest of all. He has all—even more—of Anchi's strength, greater skill in composition and design, and a girl who stands among the loveliest in ukiyo-e. Be that as it may, his pupil Anchi must be counted among the artists who never quite found their true field. Of his work in the witty genre scene of daily life in the "fleeting world," we have only that rare screen; of his prints we have only part of a set issued for some rare occasion.

It must be added that we are at something of a disadvantage in discussing the prints of the Kaigetsudo artists. With practically any other major print artist of the Edo period we have the advantage of hundreds of prints and book illustrations, most of them readily datable and extending over a period of many years, during which we may easily trace the development of the artist. With the three Kaigetsudo print designers we have only a few prints each, these designed in two or three groups, possibly at the same time, or at least within a year or so of each other. Nor is there any way to ascertain that year either: the notation "ca. 1714," usually

Plate 34. UNSIGNED: COURTESAN
Shimizu Naoji Collection.

Obviously based on Ando's famous painting of Plate 17, this work seems closest to the style of his pupil Anchi. The design of red sails behind pale-blue pine trees forms a rare and intriguing pattern.

Plate 35. TAKIZAWA SHIGENOBU: SEATED COURTESAN

Takeuchi Kimpei Collection.

Shigenobu, one of the most skilled of the later Kaigetsudo pupils, in his works shows a particular fondness for this composition, of a seated courtesan combing her hair. (Compare text, pp. 85–86.).

found in Western books on the subject, is simply an arbitrary assignation, doubtless based on the fact that this, the year of Ando's exile, is the only definite date in the whole history of the school.

III. KAIGETSUDO DOSHIN. Of the work of Doshin (Noritatsu or Noritoki), second pupil of Ando to be discussed here, we possess about fifteen paintings, but only three prints. Doshin's women are characterized by a certain mien of quiet detachment that is reminiscent of the master Ando, though lacking his depth of psychological insight. In most of Doshin's paintings the faces do not succeed in the competition for attention with the brilliant robes. In the painting of Plate 23, which is perhaps the strongest of Doshin's compositions, a certain balance is achieved by the employment of the unusual cap. The expression of retiring coyness on the courtesan's face (unfortunately lost in reproduction) is also unusual in Doshin, and gives the painting an individuality of mood that is rare in this artist's work.

Plate 25, the other signed work of Doshin reproduced, is, as we have noted there, a problem work. If genuine, it is a rare painting of Doshin's last years, dating some twenty years after his other extant work. Plate 38, with its massive, rather ungraceful figure, is typical of another phase of Doshin's style and may be tentatively attributed to him. (Like the other Kaigetsudo artists, Doshin varied between one of several styles; these may, of course, represent different periods of his career, but on the basis of the few works remaining, all undatable, it is difficult to make any categorical hypothesis at the present.)

Coming to Doshin's prints, we experience quite another impression again. We still note a certain ponderousness, a tendency of the figure to weigh down the face. But in contrast to the paintings, where the blue-gray pigments used for the delicate facial features tend to recede (and must be retouched to show up in miniature reproduction), and the brilliant reds and browns of the kimono tend to dominate, reduction of the whole to black masses and lines tends to unify the composition, and strike a happy balance between the kimono and the girl. Plates 6 and 9 well display Doshin's powers as a print designer.

We have already given our impression of Anchi's prints as being rather superior to his paintings. In the case of Doshin, the same cannot be stated categorically; perhaps we may say that his talents as a painter and a print designer are rather evenly matched. But we must add that the two forms create quite a different mood, and the gentle, unimposing grace of Doshin's paintings can hardly compete with the boldness of the prints for the attention of the hurried modern viewer. The paintings, after all, were made to be hung and viewed at leisure in the quiet alcove of some stylish eighteenth-century connoisseur; we moderns would have difficulty in recreating such ideal conditions for their enjoyment.

IV. KAIGETSUDO DOSHU. Doshu (Noritane), of whose work only six paintings, and no prints, are known, must be ranked as one of the finest of Ando's pupils. In the best of his paintings, such as that reproduced in Plate 27, he fully equals the work of the master. A close examination of his women will, it is true, reveal the lack of that indefinable spark of psychological insight that characterizes the best of Ando's work. Yet (though his extant works are few) Doshu seems to me the most consistently dependable of Ando's immediate pupils. In a painting such as that of Plate 27, he achieves a kind of distant, respectful intimacy, that comes close to the perfection of Ando's masterpiece in Plate 17. Had Doshu's work extended to the field of prints, one feels that he, like Ando, might have rivalled Kiyomasu and Masanobu in the depiction of a feminine grace that knows no boundaries of time or country.

V. KAIGETSUDO DOSHIU. The works of Doshiu (Norihide), the fifth member of the Kaigetsudo group, are now

Plate 36
BAIYUKEN KATSUNOBU:
COURTESAN. *(See Plate 28
for detail in color)*

Plate 37
TOSENDO RIFU: COURTESAN
(See Plate 29 for detail in color)

Plate 38
UNSIGNED: COURTESAN
Yamaji Shonosuke Collection.

Plate 39
KAIGETSUDO DOHAN: COURTESAN
Tokyo National Museum.

A robust composition, the oblique lines of the outer garment (slipped from the right shoulder) contrasting with the heavy outlines of the figure. Probably the work of Kaigetsudo Doshin.

Though this painting recreates something of the majesty of Ando's work, it lacks the fine taste, the hint of hidden potentialities, that are evident in the master's women.

extant in only about three paintings, no prints. Due to the similarity of name in romanization, he has usually been lumped together in Western studies with Doshu, noted above. Though Doshiu's extant works are few, they rank with Doshu's in their consistency of excellence. The painting of Plate 26, though unfortunately in poor condition, shows something of Doshiu's imposing, yet graceful style. His women display a detached yet withal forceful mien which places them in the lineage of Ando and Doshu, rather separate from the feline women of Anchi, the recessive, passive women of Doshin.

VI. KAIGETSUDO DOHAN. Dohan (Norishige), the last of the immediate pupils of Ando, was the least skillful as a painter, but produced the most prints. Only about nine of his paintings are extant, but we know fully twelve of his prints. Dohan's paintings, that in Plate 39, for example, are not particularly distinguished. They display a certain stiffness and lack of freshness and "lift," notable even in a school where originality of pose was not the main concern.

Dohan's prints are again another matter. We possess a sufficient quantity of his prints that we can be critical; and indeed, the average level of Dohan's prints is below that of Anchi and Doshin in inspiration and liveliness. Such, for example, is the print shown in Plate 10, which, though pleasant enough, and displaying a certain uniqueness of design in the use of the poem card and the bridge-landscape on the kimono, can hardly be termed a masterpiece. Again, in Plates 11 and 12 we see the pleasant, but somehow uninspired quality that characterizes most of Dohan's prints. Having said that much, however, we must turn to Plate 3, one of the loveliest in the whole Kaigetsudo canon. In this print (which we are fortunately able to reproduce in nearly half its original size) the essence of the Kaigetsudo school is somehow distilled in the work of one of its lesser members. The pose itself is somewhat improbable, but to this fact we are rendered blind by the perfection of the balance. Dohan, a painter of no particular genius, here achieves greatness through simply following, in a moment of rare inspiration, the dictates of his tradition.

Here ends our account of the Kaigetsudo group as such. Although it requires a good deal of experience to distinguish one Kaigetsudo pupil from another, the works of the founder Ando are seen to be clearly individual creations, mirrored only imperfectly even in the best of his pupils. Ando's characteristic women are strong and majestic, aloof and inscrutable, of another world. Yet even in Ando himself we find another type of girl, human and eminently approachable. Both of these types we discover mirrored in the works of his pupils; sometimes, indeed—especially in the prints—the girls of Ando's pupils may be more appealing as individual girls, as objects of the viewer's personal taste. As art objects, they are most often on a lower level than the master's—less powerful, less thoughtful, more of this world.

Although we know nothing of Ando's actual training, certain influences are clearly evident in his work. Most important, of course, is that of Moronobu and his pupils, notably Moroshige and Sugimura. The works of the Kyoto illustrators Yoshida Hambei and Omori Yoshikiyo will also bear comparison with the early Kaigetsudo paintings. From the details of these masters' works Ando perhaps learned the basic pattern of his style. Again, the genre courtesan paintings of the mid seventeenth century might well be considered the direct inspiration for Ando's majestic female figures. The influence of Ando's younger contemporaries Kiyonobu, Kiyomasu, Masanobu, and Choshun may also be cited, though they probably learned more from Ando than they taught him. Given, however, the fact of the standing figure of the courtesan (or actor) as the basic pattern of ukiyo-e, from the earliest period to the end, it is difficult to point out

Plate 40
RIFUDO KAMPU: COURTESAN
Terada Shoichi Collection.
(See text to Plate 29.)

Plate 41
MATSUNO CHIKANOBU:
COURTESAN
Tsuchiya Nanyu Collection.
(See text to Plate 30.)

what we could call evidence of decisive influence on Ando by other artists. Ando was not, of course, simply attempting to be original: he painted his girls as he imagined girls should be, basing his vision both upon the actual models then living, and upon the traditional Japanese *Yamato-e* eye that he, as a natural artist, had been born with. His vision happened to coincide with that of the connoisseurs of womanhood of his day, and his success was both immediate and natural.

LATER PAINTERS IN THE KAIGETSUDO MANNER. Although we here close our account of the immediate members of the Kaigetsudo group, there remain to be discussed the painters of the mid eighteenth century (none of whom are known to have produced prints) who exhibit a marked degree of Kaigetsudo influence. Though nominally unrelated, some of these painters were possibly pupils of the later Kaigetsudo artists; all of them owed much of their style to that created by Ando a generation or more earlier.

I. TOSENDO RIFU. A representative work of Rifu, of whom some seven paintings are known, will be found in Plates 29 and 37. Of the painters influenced by the Kaigetsudo manner, Rifu perhaps mirrors the style most accurately. His women resemble most those of Anchi, with their rather self-satisfied expressions. One does not, however, feel any great attraction toward them as women; whatever the actual age of the girl represented, she is almost matronly. Although our evidence is largely stylistic, Rifu may well have begun work around the 1720's, while the later Kaigetsudo pupils were still active.

II. TAKIZAWA SHIGENOBU. Shigenobu, whose work I have seen in some nine examples, seems to me the finest of the artists who followed directly in the tradition of the Kaigetsudo painters. He maintains the majestic grace of the early masters, while contributing a certain freshness of expression of his own devising. We see an example of his work in Plate 35, which bears his seals but not his signature.

The painting is unusual for this school in that it depicts the courtesan in deshabille—wearing only the thin *yukata* put on after the bath. Note also that her legs are crossed and her feet hidden, the latter playfully entangled in the gown's skirt. Since it is obvious that she has not a stitch on under the bathrobe, this detail may well represent a muffled hint of eroticism, rather than the expression of modesty it might at first seem. Shigenobu obviously had a fondness for this unusual seated pose, for fully half of his extant works exhibit it. His paintings show several points in common with Katsunobu, to be mentioned next, and they may well have been associates, or pupil and teacher, Shigenobu probably being the older of the two.

III. BAIYUKEN KATSUNOBU. The work of Katsunobu is discussed in the text accompanying Plate 28.

IV. MATSUNO CHIKANOBU. Chikanobu, who often used the studio name Hakushoken, is known to us in some twelve paintings; he appears to have been one of the most popular painters of his day. We see his work here in Plates 30 and 41, where a further discussion will be found.

V. BAIOKEN EISHUN. Eishun (Nagaharu), of whom over fourteen paintings are known, ranks with Chikanobu as among the most popular painters of his day. We have not been able to include his work in this little volume, but his painting style resembles greatly that of Chikanobu, and the two were perhaps in some way associated. (Eishun's studio-name, Baioken, would also seem to indicate some direct relationship with Katsunobu, whose studio was named Baiyuken.) Eishun's courtesans are tall and slim, and bear on their faces an expression rather more serious than those of Chikanobu. These two artists might be considered the center of a kind of "Kaigetsudo revival" that characterizes one important element of Edo painting during the third and fourth decades of the eighteenth century.

Among other artists, not represented in this volume but

displaying marked Kaigetsudo influence, should be mentioned the following, whose works are often known only in single examples, and among whom are doubtless to be found gifted amateurs who only dabbled occasionally in the painting of beautiful girls:

KUMEIDO NOBUYUKI, whose rare paintings might well pass for the least inspired work of Ando's pupils, in style perhaps closest to Doshin in his heavier manner.

TAKEDA HARUNOBU, a fairly early Kaigetsudo pupil, in style perhaps closest to Eishun.

KANO RYUSEN, who combines the heavy sensuality of Dohan with the archness of Anchi.

RYUUNSHI SHIGEYOSHI, whose style features refined girls with rather ungainly figures—somewhat in the manner of Eishun or Shigenobu.

RYUSENDO SHIFU, who, as both his name and style imply, was probably a direct pupil of Tosendo Rifu, displaying a style lighter, and in some ways more pleasant than his master's.

SEMMODO TOSHINOBU, an artist whose courtesans display a rather masculine mien, combined with a stance reminiscent of Chikanobu.

BORYOKEN (also pronounced Banryuken), who exhibits a graceful style of his own, perhaps closest to the manner of Shigenobu.

NOBUFUMI, a painter in the stolid, matronly manner of Rifu.

KENGETSUDO, whose naive manner is reminiscent of Katsunobu, though without his grace.

OGAWA HARYU (Haritsu), 1663–1747—the most noted lacquerware designer of his age—painted, half as a hobby, some of the loveliest *bijin-ga* of the eighteenth century. Haryu was nominally a pupil of Hanabusa Itcho, but in his ukiyo-e work he displays considerable Kaigetsudo influence. His painting, which (though highly eclectic) almost deserves standing as a school by itself, ranks among the finest done under the partial influence of the Kaigetsudo style.

HISHIKAWA MASANORI, though nominally of the Moronobu school, displays an even greater allegiance to the Kaigetsudo style, delineating a face that seems almost a parody on the feline manner of Anchi.

YOSHIKAWA MASANOBU, on the other hand, though usually treated among the Kaigetsudo artists, displays considerable skill as a painter in the Moronobu manner, with only minimal influence of the Kaigetsudo—with whom, indeed, he was probably an early contemporary.

Two artists remain to be mentioned who, though usually considered as in the Kaigetsudo tradition, are actually rather closer to the style of Sukenobu, and may well be painters of Kyoto, rather than Edo.

RYUKADO SHIGENOBU paints in the later Sukenobu manner, but with a certain grandeur of form that may well derive from the Kaigetsudo style.

NISHIKAWA TERUNOBU is a minor artist, whose work is shown and described at Plate 31.

We have made no attempt to date each of the individual painters of the Kaigetsudo school—indeed, an impossibility at the present time. Still, it is clear that the group of Ando and his immediate pupils must have flourished about the years 1700–25, and their followers in the style, ca. 1720–50. In all, then, the total life of the Kaigetsudo contribution to ukiyo-e would seem to have lasted about a half-century.

Yet ukiyo-e was never to be the same after the appearance of Kaigetsudo Ando. He created an overpowering ideal of feminine beauty that was to linger somewhere in the mind of every perceptive male who ever saw his work—an ideal that has since passed far beyond the seas, to men for whom the vision of these timeless, solitary figures sometimes seems more real than life itself.